To Ly, _ D__k_

CW01401985

Art is a Waste of Time:

Poetry Collection

Hope You enjoy this book!

Zarina Macha

Zarina ⌣

xxx

23/05/2019

For Ona and Sia, my wonderful siblings

Contents

- A-Z list of poems from 2013-2018

  Angel Face
  Art is a Waste of Time
  Beautiful Curse
  Bubble
  Cold
  Companion
  Concave not Convex
  Confusion and Uncertainty
  Dark Horse
  Dead Girl Walking
  Dear Diary
  Dear God
  Death is Peaceful
  Die, Aniraz, Die
  Distraction
  Electra and Intrama
  Familia
  Fever
  Fe-Wail
  Gentle
  Goddess
  Graduation
  Hello Toilet
  Houndog
  I can't sleep
  If I died

If you read my poetry
Interruption
Introspective Introvert
Laughter
Lovesick Longing
Mirror Mirror
My Body
My World
No More Misery
On the Train to York
Our Memories
Out, Damned Spot!
Paint a Picture
Piff Lightie
Pink Sweat
Porcupines and Concubines
Queen Bee
Reanne
Return of the Empty
Romance is Dead
Secrecy
She Grew Up
Slimy Toad
Something like affection
Splitting Headache, Broken Glass
Static Engine
Swimming (Kuogelea)
The Cleaner Comes to Town
The Narcissist
The Sea
There's BLOOD on my sheets!

Time is the enemy
Too Young
Turn Back Time
Vinz was curt and earnest
Virginity
Water
Why do we write poetry?

- Poems I wrote as a child in 2007

    Bedtime
    I badly need the toilet
    Pure Torture
    Red Hot Anger!
    Sam
    Why does everyone hate me so?

- Author's Note

Angel Face

There once was a man with locks shining gold
He approached a van, for feeling bold
Asking for great secrets on lock
Reply did sigh 'reveal I cannot'

The man entered the world of daunting doom
At his own risk, witnessed the gloom
Shudders and shouts and cries of surprise
Pain to some, but pleasure in his eyes

Smacks and swings and sweat dripped down
Thick muscles tousled, mouths in a frown
A bubble of choked release and pride
To be a real man, off the shore and pride

Shoved onto the platform of truth untold
A provocative look, spit leapt and hold
Toss onto the sheen of the man's smooth skin
Till pleasure dissolved, but he could not win

And now the man's features drip with scarlet
blood
His eyes bulging out like that of a pug
To destroy something beautiful like fair Lenore
And now Angel Face was beautiful forever no
more.

26th April 2015

Art is a waste of time

Art is a waste of time, my dear
It bears no financial gain
You shall be crippled and withered and shrivelled
Your talents down the drain
Don't waste your time with art, my dear
You are only seventeen
With your whole life laid out ahead of you
(whatever that does mean.)
Art is a waste of time, my dear
It won't make you any money
And that is the most important thing in life
More so than finding a honey.
Art is a waste of time, my dear
Those strums are good for fun
But you'll never make a living out of singing
or pouring out satirical puns.
Art is a waste of time, my dear
So cart your dreams to the shelf
Leave them stored and waste more time
Doing something else.

5th July 2015

Beautiful Curse

(Heavens; why can't I be pretty like her?)
They whisper among the shadows.
(Masses of ringlets, soft skin, model nose)
Words trail around the bushes.

(She must have men fawning over her
With a figure like that and flawless face
Radiating beauty effortlessly
No make-up needed; she's stunning).

A beautiful woman is a thing of desire
She glitters; dearest shiksa goddess.
Other eves long to possess her charms
Adams simply long to possess her.

She appears so carefree and enchanting
That stunning mademoiselle
Smiling into every mirror
Such a wonderful little belle.

Yet underneath the smiles
Tears try not to break within
That exquisite vision of perfection
Crafted; poised at the rim.

A man sees a beautiful woman
Observes Odette's grace
'From a little ugly duckling
Grew a swan with a sexy face.'

But Odette looks on; puzzled
'What else?' she asks; not of pride
But of fear disgust and anguish
Do they see nothing else inside?

Oh sure, the girl is beautiful
Any man will have her in his bed
But inside his heart? Heck no!
You'd have to look deeper instead.

Deep inside, deep inside; what's underneath?
Is beauty only skin deep?
Do you see her quirks and loves?
What makes her laugh or weep?

Can you look past the pretty face
Ignore the hourglass curves
And enter this lady's heart
To give her what she deserves?

Beautiful women don't need adoration
We need not hear we are perfect
All we need is truth and integrity
Someone to think she is worth it.

For the swan may seem captivating
Its wings are spread out wide
But that duckling still cowers down under
Desperately trapped inside.

Do you see the woman underneath?

Inside, inside, deep inside
Or simply crave the beautiful goddess
To parade around like a prize?

You may love the beauty that surfaces
Look into her eyes; do you see?
That aching hole within
The woman she longs to be.

(God, look at that ugly woman
She looks like utter shit
Her eyebrows are bushy, hair greasy;
What the hell is she wearing?

A girl like that won't find a man
He can't see what's underneath
Can't tell if she has breasts or pec's
Since her jumper covers everything!)

Brienne of Tarth was no beauty
Unlike Cersei Lannister.
Cersei's beauty was captivating
And Jaime adored her.

But Brienne's beauty was hidden
Underneath that plain bland skin
Jaime had to dig deeper
To find the beauty within.

Cersei may have been ravishing
But she lacked integrity

Brienne, on the other hand was bold
And her heart spread to the Free Cities.
A Cersei may captivate any man
Who need not work too hard
Her looks are enough to get it up
To keep him entertained; in charge.

A Cersei is a beauty
together they'll have fun
But after a while, all is lost
The man realizes he is done.

So swept up by the surface
There was no time to see
'Do I really want this woman?
Is she the one for me?

Or do I just want her looks
To hold her in my arms
To walk down the street with a stunner
And feel like the Master at Arms?

But a Brienne requires patience
Her looks are not a distraction
Since they are non-existent
He probes deeper in his attraction.

Deeper within; what's there?
What's there so deep within?
He opens up and realizes
She is the woman for him.

So yes, while it's nice to be beautiful
To be content as a Cersei
It also means that sadly
There is little else to see.

For a man may say he adores you
When he simply loves to gaze
Upon in wondrous wonder
At your pretty face

And a woman coughs and despises
You have the looks she craves
Or she thinks you're some kind of hero
For waltzing in her grace

Beauty is a dazzling gift
But Beauty is also a curse
And let it be known there may be more
Than the shining face of hers.

16th July 2018

Bubble

I wish I could stay forever in this bubble
bathed in a fuzzy glow
where my knees are sore and my mouth is dry
soothed with the gush of liquid
where my arms move of their own accord
feet following in two-step time
where my ears are buzzing with the blast of beats
the smile never leaves my face.

20th March 2016

Cold

It takes you over, consumes you
Like the elephant in the room
I'd rather be in sunny sangria
Than in the freezing land of Glassworld
It pierces through my skin like a thousand needles

My pores smashed to smithereens
The heat is never hot enough
I need more
I need it to take me over, to distract
me from the draught for which

I am not used to
I can't handle you
Go away
Get out
Get away from me

Leave me to swelter in heat.

2013

Companion

His smile puts my sorrows to sleep
We giggle like tiny children
His cuddles are softer than a gentle breeze
On a stifling summer's day.

My dearest companion, partner in crime;
You make everyday worth living.
At times your insolence infuriates
But the sea waves wash it away.

Without you my life turns to dust
It shatters into the sand
To be stamped over by rushing crowds
And children building yellow castles.

In the light of the orange sunset
Glowing its wisdom upon us
I look at you in pools of neon
And all becomes clear.

My dear, forever is a long time
It stretches out to the stars
And I will not stop loving you
Until the sun sets in the east.

When my body fades and decays
My bones cease to clench
And the last flower glides to the ground
And the seagulls stop their songs

Only then will my love float
Away into those carbons
That we came from until forming
As flesh in our mother's womb.

First I tumbled; later you came
I kissed your tiny forehead
And I knew I would always have someone
To love from hereafter.

So I say, my dearest companion
Your existence is a blessing
My heart is eternally open
For you to come home and be cherished.

21st August 2018

Concave not convex

was all that was said, and yet
your mind sparked. You wandered. You debated
and pondered.
I was beckoned, so and forth, I knew what was
coming.
My naivity in fact none existent
I know more than you thought.

All that was said
concave not convex
it sparked confusion, made you wonder, ask me
later.
I was told to keep guard, keep reserved
Hard to do when your minds flies as free as a
butterfly

Not a world in a cave
And yet I wonder,
was there a touch of non-innocence in the words
concave not convex? Who knows.

2013

Confused Uncertainty

As lightning struck the tower
His hands were cupped to his mouth.
"I have to tell you about the future!"
"I have to tell you about the future!"

To know one's future can be dire
When will I die? Marry? Pro-create?
What shall become of me?

Let's focus on the present rather than the future.
Today.
Today I am here.
Just for today.

Where do I go from here?
So many choices.
Sing my way to stardom?
Hope an agent wants my book?
Make money writing a blog?

Which way; right or left?
For sure; all paths lead to the same place.
The destination is certain; the journey is not.

Are we in this together or am I dragging them
with me?
Do they want this for real or is this just my thing?
With me or behind me; who knows?
I know we're all heading the same way.

Time; it moves so fast.
Faster than the speed of light.
Time is hard to measure.

Tick tick tick tick

We're in the same direction; all experience is
good.
I am this world and I am my experiences.
I am these colours, these words, these people.
I am the vibrations of the earth.

I am, I am, I am.

11th May 2017

Dark Horse

In the light of the shallow moon, wolves call to
howl
they stand, facing proud, tails pointed, tip of sky
swirling its frosty vanilla cloud
stop to stare, to what, to wonder -
what larks! There, on its swift cavalier back, stands
a dark horse
the hound of a huntsman lies upon it
body shrouded in mystery
eyes as bright as they are downcast
head turns away for fear or fright
and it runs into the night.

4th October 2015

21

Dead Girl Walking

This thin white noose hangs around the neck of
shame
Play your cards right as you trample towards the
hall of fame
If Venus was a goldfish she'd sparkle like Soul
Train
As his sounds sweep the slumbers of a hooded
girl's pain.

Fasten your seatbelts as you hit this ride of
crooning life
Daunting in the shadows is the echo of glooming
plight
As the days pour into numbers ticking on a
sharpened knife
Don't let the howling owl harden your reluctant
strife

Pounding on the slippery tides of relentless
desperation
Muscles ache in this glimmer of boiling
perspiration
Cut into the cheek of the skull's rash frame
She's a dead girl walking, and her screams bear no
name.

6th June 2015

Dear Diary

Dear Diary

anyone who begins a diary entry

with dear diary

is a fool

and I should like

to punch them in the face.

No, I'm joking.

Dear Diary

how I must bore you
with relentless

endless

simultaneous

moans and groans and repeat

23

repetition

round and round like a broken record
                              broken record
                              broken record
                              broken record
                              broken record
                              broken record

the same sentences chewed up in different ways
                    words spilled onto a page

Dear diary,
          what would I do without you.

9th July 2015

Dear God

Dear God,
where were you when I needed you?
when I faced verbal torment?
when my chest was too small?
Where were you when your African-American
children
were being shackled and bound? Lynched and
beaten?
Where were you when the wall that divided
East and West Germany
cut into the lives of hungry peasants?
Where were you when Hurricane Katrina
swept away families and children's toys?
I didn't see Noah's so-called-Ark
when the Tsunami smite its wonders
against those who cried and begged for mercy
and where were you when streamlined planes
crashed into the Towers of grandeur
and traumatized the world over?
Where are you every single day
millions die from hunger and AIDS
whilst the ravishing Capitol laps their pain?
When children of China and Vietnam
cast their bleeding fingers to create
branded trainers? Bags? T-Shirts?
so that a boy is not laughed at by his mates
or perhaps to save him from being stabbed?
Tell me God, where were you when that woman
was raped

and Whitney's life was taken by crack cocaine?
I could go on and on all day
but I think I know the answer, God,
is that you were nowhere

because you are not real.

　　　　Sincerely, an atheist.

9th July 2015

Death is peaceful

Sometimes, I lay back and wonder
in awe of the striking blue sky
wondering, what it would be like
to never think again
never toss and turn again
never howl inside again
simply drift off, fade away
disappear with only ink left behind
be gone from this foul world
clustered with polluted imagery
simulations one-click away
to disappear forever
simply fade away.

10th July 2015

Die, Aniraz, Die

Carved knife, crafted to a mesh of horror
Slit the throat of a red coiled pillar
If the tremor of my glimmer was the glow
then come hither, alas it is time to cry

Die, Aniraz, die, jump in front of a river
Swim forever, let crocodiles slither
Rain pours to wash away the scum
from a bleeding slither of chewing gum

Wheels grind across, sparks howl and shriek
Leap into the traffic, let the legs unwind
Arms toiling over the grey of ground
Dismal smack, with barely a sound

Polish the revolver, shine its sheen slick now
Lick tongues over the trigger as it crows
sneering and sliding, every last pull
Tiny fingers, they heave and they haul.

26th April 2015

Distraction

When you're in school and study hard
A boyfriend is just a distraction.
When you're at uni getting life together
A boyfriend is just a distraction.

When you're scraping to get the career all set
A boyfriend is just a distraction.
When you make it big touring round the world
A boyfriend is just a distraction.
When you're sitting at home answering calls
A boyfriend is just a distraction.

When...

When they ask why you don't have a man
You say 'I don't need a distraction.'
When you're crying in your room all alone at night
At least you don't have a distraction.
When your friends are in couples and you're
focused on yourself
At least you have no distractions.
When their kids are playing and you're hard at
work, hey;
Children are just a distraction.

When you're lying in bed and time passes by
At least you don't have a distraction.
When your deathbed is coming and its time to
end

I lived life without a distraction.

14th November 2016

Electra and Intrama

With each passing slap of wind
There sings a walking contradiction
I ask, the dear Gemini twins
One resonates with sonorous laughter
Ready to bow to all who witness
Prance with Chaplin's footsteps
And glide freely in ecstasy.
The other, so gloomy and dull
Yet with a heart that shines so pure
Succumb to the quench of poison
And reach for loathsome self-pity.
Who is the one who holds the most
Can one be two, and two be whole
Can hairs on the back of necks be traced
By both which sounds and is gazed
And can she glide into the chowder
As it burns in holy grail
Held so tender, so dear, like flour
moulded into shapes like so
echoing direct personas.

5th July 2015

Familia

Mi padre es fenomenal;
Mi madre también.
Creo que tengo suerte
Por bueno relación con mis padres
No gentes todas tienen buenos relaciones
Con su familia.

Mi hermano es mi favorita
Persona en el mundo.
Mi hermana es muy guapa
En dentro y fuera.
Tengo muchos primos y tíos
Y mi abuela siempre estoy feliz.
Además, mi prima...

¿Prima?
Hola, prima.
¿Como estas?
Porque tú habla cosas malas
Acerca de 'favorita' prima.

Escucha, mi amor
Fui tu amiga preferida.
Pues, es claro ahora
La amistad debe terminar.

¡O, soy exagerativo!
¿Pero qué cosa tu odio su prima?
No es información correcto

Ahora habla en todo recto.

Seis de Julio 2018

Fever

Fever makes you sick.
Fever makes you hot.
Fever makes you sweat.
Fever makes you drip
tremble
quake with nerves and desire
Fever comes as quick as its gone
Fever is for now.

For now, and you were my first
My first fever
For now, and you were my first
Choking on your own fever.
Catch the fever
I nearly caught yours

You nearly gave me your fever
You nearly gave me your sickness
You nearly gave me your pain
Aches and illness and tears and pain
Your fever was nearly my fever

But I wanted your fever and you were my first
Your fever struck me and you were my first
At first the fever did not seem to be there
But as it got hotter things began to flair
and fever gets hotter the longer it lasts
The longer its left untreated it lasts
Treat your fever before I catch it

don't give your fever to me.

But I wanted your fever
Craved
Gasped
Burnt
Burnt for your fever
Fever is contagious, infectious
I nearly caught your fever
I nearly caught your fever and you were my first
You will always be my first fever.

2nd July 2016

Fe-Wail

Pain.
Ripping hair out of body, tearing away.
Flesh.
Smooth, silky flesh, heaven between my legs.
Flesh, soft as feathers, long and lean and sexy
Sexy legs.
Rip flesh, pluck, tweezer, wax, thread
Beauty is pain
Rip flesh, so I can be beautiful like an Ann
Summers model.

Pain.
Every month she waves her wand
Drown in your own blood
(Red rum)
Cries. Pills and painkillers, put her to rest
Why.
Mother nature, why would ya, make us drown in
our blood once a month?
Aches, oooh, stabbing in the stomach
Punches over and over again

Pain.
(Ssh baby, it's ok just relax)
Penetration.
Blood everywhere...
(But I want you)
OUCH!
Stabs in the crotch, penis tearing me apart

Rip.

Rip through a girl's virginity as she clutches onto
you for dear life
OW.

Pain.
A new life from the old, our main purpose
Pro-create.
Woman breathes life, woman bears life
Womans bears pain of bearing life.
SCREAMS
DOCTOR HELP ME OH HELP ME SO
DOCTOR DOCTOR I THINK I'M DYING

Pills and painkillers, painkillers and pills
C-Section.
(Pain is too grand)
A woman's pain as she wails
As her man holds her hand, holds her body,
Holds her hair back as she vomits
Strokes her when she's sick
Listens to her screams and demands
Nods his head without wail.

Without response to a woman's wails.

23rd June 2016

Gentle

Softly does her tone go
sweet and breathy, light as wire
hair glistening, wiry black curls
framing unusual features
pretty in orange free-spirit
lain back, arching silver birch
grass tickling tender feet
brows arched; no pushover is she;
humble, not meek
a warm-hearted tender streak
chatter soothes my skin
puts me right at ease
laid down flat on this ground
squatted under the towering tree
dewy wonder; cycle round
I beckon thee.

10th July 2015

Goddess

Tall, and slender, bubbling with life
She turns heads with a swish of her pride
Revelling in creamy white and chocolate brown
With almond and hazel fluttering around

Delicate like the touches of piano
Trembling within a smudge of mulatto
Flattened against the rims of her skin
As she cries and stumbles against starched
porcelain

A childlike waver of naivety breathes
Upon a trickle of darkening ease
That gathers up towards each plight
And plunges itself down off the night

But still she holds her head on a plume
That shivers and sings to conceal inner doom
Sheer grace shines free to hit all sky
And casts its legs on yonder high

So smite those shards of crumbling tears
'Daddy, you bastard!' she cries without fear
Yet curl up to the tenacious blow
Of inner beauty that kisses her woe

Shall dance until the break of dawn
And swallow the humble shears that swarm
For magical is this wondrous gift

Of the girl who gazes at me with bliss.

7th July 2015

Graduation

So proud as we watched you as you strolled down
swaggering, head cocked
so proud as you walked, strolled, smiled
so proud I am, as you banged those drums
bang bang one time for me
so proud, as you kept the beat
guitar in hand, little hendrix
so proud, hands in admiration
stature lean and strong
not the biggest of fellows, but big-hearted
smile makes my cheeks melt
dearest companion, from little-uns
throwing stuffed cats and dogs about
naming, gaming, shaming, our fights
not every minute a total delight
but still, I shall not knock you down
our laughter a song not to be destroyed
together a force to be reckoned with
as I look now, at you young man
so proud
how you have grown.

10th July 2015

Hello Toilet

Hello Toilet,
                    we meet again.

How tired you must be of me!

Time to drip-drop-dump
the chewed up beast that was yesterday's joy
beer
chocolate
cake
pizza
perfect fried chicken

Oh toilet, I'm sorry I abandoned my parent's
warns
I'm sorry I could not resist the call of sugar
empty food for an empty heart

But toilet, as we are now friends,
                                        tell
me this

Why do I see blood?

9th July 2015

Houndog

High in the mountains of East Africa
The Hound dog barks and howls.
He calls on the world to listen
To his witty words of wisdom.

He prances from rock to rock
Making the others gaze in wonder
At this dashing young creature
Brimming with bright charisma.

His tail is cocked to attention
His eyes shine with readiness
More and more animals come to listen
To what this dog is about.

The ladies smile and swoon
At this dog's enticing ways.
He's a hound dog; tramp, a rover,
And they all want to travel his way.

He's got them by the ear
Telling them tales of his adventures
Music, fashion, art and colours
A world he painted over.

The hound dog is a wise one
He says life is for living.
Don't waste the time you have here,
For it will past by quickly.

This hound dog is not perfect
His fur is rugged and worn
But not to worry, for lady still
Shares a meatball with him.

He's a hound dog alright; a tramp,
A rover, and a scoundrel.
Very wise, full of life and colour,
I wish that I could travel his way.

11th May 2017

I can't sleep

I'm a prisoner trapped in my own body
Locked away, waiting for sleep to take me
My rumpelstiltskin, my loan shark
The one I depend on continues to deceive me

I lie awake, letting the tide of drowsiness wash
over me
My brain fired up, electrons racing, charging
I wonder, while the rest of the world lies like logs
I am banished to the horrors and chills of my own
mind

Unable to distinguish between what is real and
what isn't
My subconscious as hectic as my conscious
Aged 4, aged 7, aged 12, aged 14, aged 17
One thing in common they share
We share.

Why can't we be friends, dear sleep?
For some people they are lovers
But to me we are enemies
Sometimes I love you, sometimes I hate you
You tempt me in, pull me down
Then as soon as I think victory will be mine
I'm doomed to the contours of my own mind
I lie still.

During the day I'm frantic, energetic

Then turn to the living dead – asleep while awake
I dread those hours when I need more hours
Yet I'm wide awake. Is this real?

I can't tell if I'm dreaming or lucid
I can't tell what's real and what isn't
Am I a brain in a jar? But my legs, they stiffen
The ongoing battle, beats the battle of Britain
Why can't we just be friends, why can't we get along
Don't make me turn to the pills.

This is simply unfair, few will understand unless they
share that position of the undead.
Worse my fatigue inflicts upon me
Worse my insomnia becomes
Heavier my body gets, tenser and sorer
My mind can't write any wrongs.

14th September 2014

If I died

If I died
Would you care I was gone?
If I died.

If I stood on the cliffs of Dover
Peering down into the sea
Would you care?

For you once held me so dear
Now you despise me
Or think nought;
My name flashes, you appear non-committal

I ask; did I matter or was it a lie?

If I died
Would you come to my funeral
Would tears fall from your eyes
As you cried
While they played a song by JLS

Would you heart skip a beat?
Feel remorse or deceit?
Would it matter to you if I died?

If I cried
Weeping endlessly into the winds of winter
Carried by smokes howling among leaves
My voice launching into the distance

Clutching my throat as the noose wrapped
Its greedy hands around my neck.

If I died
Would it matter to you?
Do we value others only when no longer with us?

If I died
Would you care?
Perhaps you would do well
To value those who care for you
When they are still alive.

16th July 2018

If you read my poetry

If you read my poetry
If you heard my songs
you would understand me a lot better
than if we stood
face to face
side by side
shoulder to shoulder
you would see the cracks
in a mask so carefully built
sealed to protect a fragile heart
from tumbling down the cliff
draining a frothy waterfall
welled up a leaky dam
that mooches up and down streets
slumped into rounded shadows.

8th July 2015

Interruption

I was lying, I was laying, and my phone started braying
And your name flashed up upon my screen
I was lying, I was sighing, I was wondering and why-ing
You should seek reason to appear on my screen

And I answered and you answered and I spoke through my handset
As your voice spoke in its ever-so familiar ring
Shrill and hitting, barely singing, yes it stated for a minute
As you told me your whereabouts on the call of your ring

And I sighed, and I stared, into space, as I glared
For my ever personal soundtrack was interrupted again
And I did not want to speak for the needs that you seek
As I lay back on my self-centred comfy chair.

26th April 2015

Introspective Introvert

I am an introspective introvert
on one side of the pole
few do see
very few but me
these words that touch the paper
mutter from head to lips

I am an ambivert
claiming electric energy
and introspection

                                        inside
                                        inside
                                        inside my
mind I tunnel

                                        deep inside
                                        rich inner life
                                        sensitivity
prickles

                                        how it
trickles

                    trickles
                            trickles
                                    trickles

deep inside, the world is mine.

10th July 2015

deep inside, the world is mine.

10th July 2015

Laughter

Laughter is as laughter does
Fills room with a cheerful buzz
Cold, dull, empty, numb,
laughter counteracts the glum

Men, women, clink glasses galore,
Sitting, standing, laughs adore
Cheerless waves pile a frown
Laughter commands like a clown

Everyone is in on the joke
Laughing till their stomachs choke
Sighing, sinking, mirthless doom
Laughter covers up the gloom

In a room of merry folk
Cheerful as the highest stoke
Trapped still in flat unease
Laughter cures many-a disease.

17th November 2016

Lovesick longing

Hearts of hedonism hold hands hereafter
A tide of ecstasy could not bring one more
pleasure
You gaze, with a face, full of eternal bliss
If Heaven was real it would be your halos
Cuddled together in a warm bubble glow
Dazzling light enshrines hazel with honey
How does the flying butterfly even compare
With wings of pink that flutter in the air
Love is a gift that many do share
For some its a curse that swoops over dark hair
Grind and boil my blood till its churns
You have what I want and am yet to learn.

26th April 2015

Mirror Mirror

Mirror mirror, on the wall
who is the fairest that you see
mirror mirror, tell me who
is the reflection that you be

Do I recognize this girl
who stares back at me
torn between the ones who know
the roots that stem from their tree

Lost in a world, entirely my own
A planet within a planet
Does this resonate with my own
inner reality

Oh mirror, don't let me down
Hold me close, take care of me now
Where there is a will, there is a way
Do I walk through the reflection or walk away?

2nd September 2014

My Body

My body is beautiful.
It glides through the water, arms strong; legs
compact.
Soft yet full, it holds me.
Pear shaped breasts symbolize my womanhood
I am beautiful woman.

My legs stretch out
Brown, strong, they run
Through the woods; trees hush in awe
The wind cheers me on.

My buttox sits on his face
He holds it; feels its richness.
My body is a delicious fruit
And he is the seed inside of me.

His seed is my ecstasy
Euphoric; I howl
Our bodies are one
Moving into each other.

Let no one shame your body
Women stand in the cubicle
Undressing, unashamed
White, brown, soft, thick
Like bread unwrapped from its package
Waiting to be eaten.

When did nakedness become shame?
Underneath our clothes we are all nude
Why is the human body X-Rated
Nature's purest gift should be celebrated.

I feel my beautiful body
Move my finger down to pink pleasure button
Let them also tap out words on a keyboard
Strum guitar strings
Hold a pen
Grip the phone to call my brother
To tell him; he is beautiful
Our bodies came from the same womb
Raw and untouched
Perfect. Pure. Perfectly pure.
Yet clothes must cover up.

Tell your daughter to be ashamed of their bodies
Shame their skin
Flesh
Hair
Shame is all
Let no man fall to lust; to desire flesh is sin
(not a nutritious human need)
Cover your face, skin, hair
Or run to the toilet and purge
Burn your throat as the food erupts
From the volcano within your gut
Burn it all.

Poison your body; poison your mind

Let it slip into venomous hatred
Ignore the food; push away
This bulge on my tummy, these burns at my
breast
Scars everywhere, on arms and legs
Mutilate your body and destroy
Destroy ones' body; destroy ones' self
Let this body be cut to pieces
Burned, slashed, purged,
Until the person underneath is nought
But a black smudge waiting to be wiped.

No?

Break the cycle, my child
Free your body from its chains
Let the world see no shame
In flesh, cells and nerve-endings
Never-ending nerve-endings.

Love your body and it will love you
For your body is a delicious fruit
And I am the seed inside of you.

19th August 2018

My World

You handed me your smile, and a shake of rippling
gold
Cascading like rain in amazon; I was sold
Years have flown by, delivered innocently by the
stork
Time and time again, bundles of mirth and
merriment

Dance like the viper lurking in the bushes
A creature of forked tongue, deadly poison
Cut through the angelic exterior most blindly see
The picture of wholesome immunity

I know the truth behind the denim eyes
I see you, for you were my world
My splash of colour, fluorescent joy
Partner in crime, right hand lady

Humans epitomize imperfection, for that I am glad
Simply short, sharp words could make me mad
Or no words at all; sheer action, eye roll

And I am not flawless, no diamond in the rough
Love flows, but you make it tough
When all is said and done, the circle has no end
And that is how long I will be your friend.

22nd February 2015

No More Misery

Time to regain the loss of life
So humbly do we spring, together in chorus
Skip merrily, for summer brings its wealth
of endless golden wonders to which now shoots
up into the strums of tight coloured leggins
And the beat of a nodding cock-a-doodle-doo

Goodbye Misery, for now at least
Fairwell, no longer shall you taunt me again

Misery lived with me for a while
Perhaps growing longer than I could think
Now she jumps; I tell her take a hike
As I buzz off to sunny sistine chapel land
Dear Misery, you won't burn my works
or cut my feet
or keep me from falling asleep
Oh Misery, I am no longer afraid
No longer in pain
Demon drink is far away
For now, perhaps we shall meet again
But I hope that day shall not soon be chastained.

5th July 2015

On the train to York

A collection of green, passing
instantaneous move of time
So quick . It never existed
Same rivers, little boats ; sheep chorus happily
Clouds dance between grey and gold
A car in the distance gets further and further
I wonder, what is each and every journey?
So many roads, one final dead end.

Smoke pours out, medieval factories,
Like soldiers, hard at work
Company and companionship not difficult to find,
coming in many colours, chequered blue ,
rebellious red

Alone but never alone at all, and I wonder
What sets me apart? Writing without thinking
Although I plan to specialize in the subject of
thought
Still I wonder.

20th September 2014

Our Memories

Laughter swishing on the sofa
spin around, hands held
from here to Angel
scanning aisles for un-purchased clothing
streaming the internet for japes
sat for ages, no words said
just happy space
head on shoulder
happy was I, happy was you
happily on the merry-go-round
until I felt dizzy and ill
dizzy with the dazzle of your happy smile
building blocks of friendship
legs kicked out, a team we were!
smiles fondly stolen
as I ponder in wonder
at our collection of memories.

10th July 2015

Out, Damned Spot!

Out, Damned Spot, Out I say!
Oh, you sit and snigger
tucked on to the edge of my nose
red like a sour bittersweet rose
enigmatic as to its whereabouts
popping up on this caramel canvas
smooth no more, bumps do saturate
appear heathen upon my face
Out, Damned Spot, Out I say!
Must you crawl with little effort?
Prowling baleful amongst glands
of rolling humble dampness.

10th July 2015

Paint a Picture

Paint a picture like Pollock
Filled with abstract dots
An expression of a young man's innocent smile.
His heart filled with joy
Yet wounded with sad tears
Trailing ghosts of a mother's whisper.

Kisses warm and hungry,
Lusting with passion and desire
Bristles on his chin stroke mine soft
Marking against the chiselled jaw.

Underneath; jittering heartbeats
Felt against skin so frail
Bones meek yet robust
Without fail; he will prevail
A desire to let go and rock steady.

An enquiring mind, face of curiosity
Canvas of sensual beauty.
Poised, then turned to mirth
Like ashes fallen to earth
In a wholesome ball of kindness
Take my hand and let's fly, dear phoenix.

17th April 2018

Piff Lightie

There are no black people and there are no white
people

There is pale, ice-cold snow white, tender and
succulent
Melting into creamy-white, bordered with
strawberry smudges

Slowly dissolves into tan
Bronze-skinned
Exotic and fiery
Yellow-skinned
Red-skinned
Redbone, all the shades of non-literal red
Before slowly blending into the light-skinned piffie

The piff lightie
What is a lightie?
Smooth, creamy skin of a mixed raced person
Beautiful yellow-skinned Asian or Latina lady,
 with flowing, lustrous jet black hair

Mixed race yellow-skinned boy, darkening tones
to almost orange in the summer
A light-skinned black
Caramel skinned, delicious ice-cream

The taste of rich chocolate blossoming across your
arms

Before it burns into an even darker, richer, irresistible swirl of cocoa, the darkest, deepest, richest chocolate.

Blick.

Lightie.

Brownie.

What relevance ?

These words...

There is no lightie, just light-skinned, cream, red or yellow

Brownie?

Or are you too mixed race
Or just caramel skinned
Or just brown.

Blick?

Why be ashamed to have ebon skin; smooth and dark as truffles
Beautiful and flawless

What is that obsession

A black person wishes to be lighter
A white person wishes to be darker

Be proud of your hues and shades
relish upon it

For every colour is beautiful
Every colour should be accepted
Every colour
Every colour
Everyone.

2013

Pink Sweat

Dripping from every pore
Snatch hands away,
my palms.
"Why are your hands so sweaty?" She cries
"Why?" He cries
"That girl's hands are so sweaty!" They cry
Sly, strain, un-Freudian repression
Unreleased misery, unreleased thirst
mountain of tears.

"Don't cry" the caged owl sings.
For the ill only
Not for she who has plenty
Twiddling locks round; rapunzel is jealous.

Sweat
In Summer, weeping; narcissistic, self-
indulgent
In Winter, occurs mostly at night
Toes, soles, fingers, tips
Runny
Honey,
don't cower from hiperhidrosis.
But you will, as we fear what we don't
understand
Fear strips all rationale,

said the bespectacled literature professor
sitting at his desk.

Fear is an emotion; emotions are for the
weak,
the tough sassy girl remarked.

2014

Porcupines and Concubines

Round. Curved. Retrieved. Then release.
Smite my inner shards, until they ripple
down
Bolts of lightning on my soul.
Open wide. Then release.
Pour silky chasms of snarls and slithers
Withering away like the rose in a bed of
glass

Dreams of a companion, someone to lay
I call upon thee, who replies nay
To my shame, face flushes crimson like hair
used to be
Breath in and out, breath evades me
Right from the breaching hollows of your
scorn
Prickly like the thorn
Until I declared no more.

28th February 2015

Queen Bee

An enchantress; she summons the others in
the hive
busy from collecting sweet yellow honey
the mother hen, not the boldest but the
bravest
ready to take command of all

own a night of fertilised magic
that is sung upon flowers of all colours
red roses, purple violets, white daisies,
orange poppies
zig-zagging among prickling blades of grass
slapping them away until she desires to
enter
home to her one and only solid oak tree
with leaves branching out to kiss the sky

swirl her name among the stars
down-to-earth, resting her tired wings
still buzzing forever, stand back as she
stings
humming the world over, to the night and
beyond
all bees must leave the hive
and fly, so their honey can be shared
not to everyone's taste, but with many
made full

happy to bask in her warm glow
so rich, leaves a mark of content.

9th July 2015

Reanne

Standing at the end of the halfway line
She meets me once I give the sign
Hopeful still, was my dear mind
To catch a chat off one playtime

Tumbling spirals of secure black
Plaited with precision, all down her back
Butterscotch cheeks, innocent and raw
But sadness concealed under her jaw

Handed a heart-felt picture or two
The other girls wish to talk to you
And envy sends shocks up my spine
Quote Paul and Michael; the girl is mine

Lonesome playmates mull together
Come rain, come shine, come hither, come
never
I needed you then; how are you now?
What happened to my little Reanne.

25th May 2015

Return of the Empty

Emptiness; she returns in her ghostly image
Weaving her shadow of hollow nothingness
Chipping away at every emotion
Leaving nothing but a desire to feed.

To feed on substance; sweet substance
Sweet smoky sparkling substance
To fill up the empty once more
And replace with lethargy and fatigue.

Dear Emptiness, you ate him and now his is
mine
The nothing that plagued him seeped into
me
My thoughts of him; garnering thoughts
Thoughts of what was, could be, might have
been

He torments me in my thoughts
I wonder; am I in his? Does he care? Does
he realise?
Realise his fleeting impact has been
snatched away
Leaving nothing but a mark of empty.
An empty mark, a dark mark, a mark that
time will fade
But a mark nonetheless.

All for nothing? I wonder
People seep in and out, their words and
memories weaving
Filling our lives with colour, fleeting in and
out
Building us up or tearing us apart
Can each impact build bridges or burn
them? Can it
Create a calvary of wordly charm, bringing
us closer
Letting us hold hands and sing in this joyous
life
Or does it remind us that in the end we are
alone
Lying alone, in the casket or grave, buried
Ready to return to the nothing we once
were.

With each passing person, passing glance or
kiss or dance
Are we aware of the chains we build, tender
bonds
Or are they simply fragments in the great
prison of Oz
Fragments that make each day a reason for
getting up
Clinging onto the collective; living through
others

Trying not to collapse under the weight of it
all.

Is it all for nothing? The end is the same
None are exempt and none can avoid
Spin whatever story you like; the end is the
same
But the journey, the journey cannot be
walked alone
For man and woman were not made to be
alone

The Abrahamic God created Adam and Eve
As the Hindus sang of Rama and Sita
But before Sita, Rama was content
And before Eve, Adam did not moan when
alone
Yet their existence made their lives whole
And it is hard not to wonder.

To wonder why each day passes by
And every human is wondering the same
thing
Could part of the empty be, that Adam does
not have Eve
His life may be full and content, and yet
That hollowness cannot be hid, can't forget
When a missing piece of the puzzle is rid

Despite all that garners self-content within
Every Sita needs her Rama and still vice
versa
If not; Rama take Adam and Eve take Sita
Whichever creates happiness and builds the
bonds
Building the bonds of life.

Our one purpose; to pro-create
Pro-creation needs two, lest our species die
out
Thus that need to find another is wired
inside
When that need is unfulfilled, Empty comes
and shits
Shits all over our soul, our DNA, our self-
content

Self-contentment and joy can only take us
so far
But a point arises when it is no longer
enough
When another is needed to share that same
joy
To laugh and leap and shout to the heavens
Shout; I am happy, he is happy, our
happiness is one
But I am happy; he is sad, I am happy; she is
sad

Our fragments wither and crumble and wilt
The balance is dead and togetherness
lifeless
And leaves us both sitting underneath this
dark mark.

This dark mark of continued Emptiness.

13th August 2016

Romance is dead

Romance is dead, men are pigs,
Women are crazy narcissists
Gone are the days of wooing a lady
Pouring a heart and soul out loud
Romance is dead, marriage is over,
Divorce rate is up every day
Women now spurn every man they meet
Making them all impossible to please
Romance is dead, love is a myth
Death do part be a thing of the past
Goodbye to courting and merry young love
Drama, break-ups and cries replace
Romance is dead, our people is lost
Family is fading away every day
Babies grow up, no father figure
Daughters grow up hating their mothers
Romance is dead, humanity is doomed
Kiss goodbye to happy French kisses
All is lost in the blink of an eye
No longer is she the apple of his eye.

28th July 2016

Secrecy

I am a nightingale bound in secrecy
Like sugar wrapped in moist liquor
Unable to face the rampaged humdrum
Of a careless rush of gnarled scratches

Hold it tight to your arteries, my darling
Entrust few with this innate knowledge
For actions speak louder than words
And actions shall determine this fateful
curse

Head cocked to the side in sympathy
For the ones whose job it appears to be
To look with apparent innocent bliss
As this child speaks of her only wish.

6th July 2015

She Grew Up

Sansa gazed out the window
Waiting for the prince she was promised
A sight of golden blonde hair
And blue eyes like his mother's.

He'd whisper sweet words in her ear
Tell her she was his one and only
Together they'd ride to the sunset
On their shared white horse.

Yet as the prince stepped closer
Sansa began to notice things
His harsh jeers and laughs
Mocking all within his path

Prince Joffrey seemed so perfect
Yet why was he so arrogant?
For a brave gallant young man
He was nought but a coward

Joffrey snapped and snarled, that sadist
Discarded all he deemed inferior
Sansa's perfect dream was shattered
As she saw beneath the mask

To her horror, this shining prince
Mounted daddy's head on a stick

And so Sansa finally realised
Fairy tales do not exist

After many years of hurting
And pining for true love
Sansa learned the best love
Was there all along

She knew her true power
Was running through her veins
Little girl finally grew up
Seeing the 'prince' was her reflection.

16th July 2018

Slimy Toad

Slithering in the shadows
Lurks the slimy toad
His eyes as black as his soul

Pungent odour reeks off him
Poisoning his swamp
He sticks his tongue into the first lady toad
he sees

'Sweet lady; I have enough flies for us both'
Eager; lady toad follows this monster
Not yet knowing his true nature

Deceit is sly; 'here, eat this fly,
I shall feed us both'
says the toad.

So clever is he; yet don't you see?
The blankness in his eyes?

You disgust me, toad,
You rancid beast
It pains me deeply to think
Our bodily fluids combined as one
How my essence vomited after touching
you

Your tongue left a bitter taste in my mouth
Stench so nauseating I'm still recoiling

Unhappily how it took me so long
To realise; you can't turn a toad into a
prince
with a kiss.
Alas; you're left only with the kiss of death
If you continue to embrace toads.

18th July 2018

Something like affection

Lying on the grass, arms wrapped around
me
Lips soft and wet, they entice me
Sun beams at us in each other's arms
Nothing but the earth beneath our bodies

Kiss me, dear man, hold me tight
Protect me from many-a fright
Your body is strong and firm
I shiver at the thought of you inside me

Something like affection when you hold my
hand
Is the feeling I get when I'm with you
Something like affection when you look at
me
Your eyes, brown and beautiful

Something like affection when your lips
match mine
They intertwine; your territory marks my
mouth
Something like affection, Australian guy,
It ripples up and down my back.

Can't bring myself to look deep into those
eyes

Framed by immaculate long lashes
Laugh and smile puts me at ease
You treat life as if it's a breeze

Take all that comes within your stride
If you're knocked down it won't scar your
pride
You are life, the epitome of joy and
kindness
No bad bone in your soul.

Something like affection when I think of you
Runs through me; am I good enough for
you?
Something like affection that a real man will
give me
The treatment they say I deserve

Something like affection; we hike through
the forest
Take in mother nature's true beauty
Something like affection holds man and
woman
Together as was intended.

14th June 2017

Splitting headache, broken glass

Ice cream is sweet and berries are sour
Soft romance blithers less fanciful per hour
She looked into his pretty blue eyes
And history curled the winds that glide

Eighteen years bears short life-span
For what seems long now, later seems a
plan
Of a cardboard box of Italian jewels
And diamonds that trickle over pale hues

He seemed to resemble her whole wide
world
How happy he made her, beautiful girl
Sugar-coated sprinkles fade away
Until the true colours splurge over at bay

You see, my dear, it is ok to cry
For the night is young, yet she wonders why
A man so loving, who sang her name
Could now be causing so much pain

The fault lay within neither of the two
Just one of those things, that you daily do
Or monthly, or yearly, off on the trot
Chalk over the ground 'forget me not'

Young lovers weep at the fall of the end
Wondering how one will love again
But shortly he made her the happiest alive
And to me that is the greatest prize.

2nd May 2015

Static Engine

Oh static engine, stuck in a field of guilt
Frozen in the face of papers and markings
Walls are my witness, non-judgemental
bystander
Behind them, shakes of head are apparent

One should tend to the mountain, for it's
yet to climb
I have hit the edge of unforgiving stone
Icy, dicy, not a little bit spicy
Dabbing into my head telling me to get a
move on

Two more months, two more weeks, two
more years, two forever
two plus two makes four, to all but Orwell
If two was the magic number I'd forever
know no luck
For it seems a brick wall my brain has stuck

Time is ticking, days are hissing, lips are
kissing but mine
World of running cats and shooting sparks
prod more interest
Then these baleful mounds of paper that
greed my morning slumber
Prod my wish to tear down these walls.

26th April 2015

Swimming (Kuogelea)

Ninapenda kuogelea
Kweli, sana; maji mazuri
uzuri wa bahari ni wa Mungu
hata ingawa siamini.

Inside the sea I am free
The waves splash around me
My limbs twist and turn
Moving with the rhythm of the water.

I look to the sky and the wind
Bless me; I salute you
I am humbly yours; o' great one
The mother of all our elements.

Wind gently sprays its echoes
Whispering through my hair
The sun smiles and beams its light
The rays kiss my caramel shield

If my body were made of salt
Then my legs would turn to scales
Sequins of emerald green and silver
Sparkling with a pearly sheen.

I would sail through the oceans
A mermaid of this blue planet

Let my hair curl from head to fin
"Hello there; amber fish!"

Let us do the dance of water
Let our bodies tangle within
We don't know body from tail
Where I end and where I begin.

22nd August 2018

The cleaner comes to town

Every Sunday, bright as a buzzard
The cleaner comes to town
Here and there, from dusk till dawn
She goes wearing a frown
Scrounges of crumbs from the night before
Splashes of dirt on yonder door
Tides of water to flourish and mop
The cleaner scrubs them down
Mutters of growls sneak on the warpath
Scalpel polished ready to spike
Those pesky kids that blast the night
With their greasy stubby hands
Hustle and bustle from room to room
Ready to swish, all set to groom
Make way, ladies and gentlemen please
The cleaner is in town.

5th May 2015

The Narcissist

Gazing into the flows of the river
Stream that fatal blur of beauty
Narcissus hooted and cooed with delight
At the image of spiralled perfection

Gone was Echo, so locked in distress
Swerve daintily down only to fall
Narcissus posed no interest in her
As the image glowed without flaws

Gorgons could not distort nature's creation
Sad was Medusa at the loss of her pride
Narcissus was charmed by alluring grace
As the image shone ever-so-tantalizing

But edge closer to the sheen of splendour
Young child see not that one went under
For Narcissus tumbled into the image
That beckoned his name without words

All is not as it appears to dazzle
Don't be swayed by magnificent face
It lures deep unto murky storm
And ploughs into the shallows

Narcissism eats my sides for dinner
Washes over starch fried withered bones

Throw yourself down into the horrors
Or run before it steals all you own.

4th May 2015

The Sea

Vast and beautiful, oh mighty sea
Down here we all float too.
Carry me waves, push me ashore
Together we will float too.

Underneath the rays if you look at the sun
You will surely float too.
Basking in the glory of beautiful light
Honey, you will float too.

You'll float too under the sea
You'll float with Flounder and Ariel
Posideon will cast his mighty trident
And make sure you'll float too.

You will float, and the sea will gloat
As it proves who the true boss is.
You will float in the mighty waves
Under the sea and sunshine rays.

22nd August 2017

There's BLOOD on my sheets!

There's BLOOD on my sheets!
There's BLOOD on my sheets!
Did myself on reds; there's BLOOD on my
sheets!
He did me first time, now there's BLOOD on
his sheets!
Mother Nature did warn me, now there's
BLOOD on my sheets!

Oh poo, screw you, oh why, I cry
As I clean and scrub this BLOOD off my
sheets
Oh mummy, where are you, please help me
please
Please help me get rid of this BLOOD on my
sheets!

4th November 2016

Time is the enemy

Time is the enemy, my father did say to me
As he preened upon his own foreboding
clock
Time waits for nobody, as it ticks with each
body
Winding down to which it flows upon the
dock

Time is the enemy, ticking with each
remedy
Feeling for the gasping ache of mercy's rock
Time ticks for certain, can't hide behind the
curtain
Or sneak past the gazing wind of jaunty
Ayer's Rock

With each passing moment time shares
tick
tock
on the
clock

Don't want to be late, don't want to be
forgot

tick
tock

on the
clock

chop chop little one, chop chop.

8th July 2015

Too Young

You can't feel that at your age, you're too young.

Too young to drink
Too young to be in love
Too young to be depressed
Too young to know what you want
Too young to move out
Too young to go abroad
Too young to have sex
Too young to get married
Too young to know this
Too young to know that
Too young to be cynical
Too young to wonder if this is all bullshit

And yet, like Carrie, I couldn't help but wonder.
When do you stop being too young?

28th July 2016

Turn back time

If I could go back eighteen years
And stop you from marauding ears
Stop the conceive of baby born
Prevent each slip of waking dawn
Go back to the humble dwell of sin
Without this curious little chin
That rides up till the curving hill
And climbs up on its window sill
I wonder what her thoughts were then
So full of potential, happy as hen
To turn into this queen of sorrow
So bleak and quaking on the morrow
Yet dizzy with each tiny slip
That yearns to drink and take a sip
of raw honey tumbling from life
Streaming down into stumbling ice
So perhaps one must not make haste
To turn round and not finish the race.

8th July 2015

Vinz was curt and earnest

Vinz was curt and earnest
A rather dapper young fellow
He enjoyed carving out crafts of wonder
And sticking them on large pillows.
He poured his heart out to the maid
Who replied by looking solemn and staid
and said he needed to get laid
or clamber out of the window.
At least, that was his interpretation.
He swam around seas of golden fish
Lumbered in a school of convenience
Tossed and turning over his neurons
And making his wife be more lenient
To his stressed and strung-out demands.
He lay his head where the sun didn't shine
And strapped his lungs to the chords of
time
For they were not like yours or mine
But much much much more limited.
To take his breath and cut it short
With the scalpel that renewed his thought
And on the canvas he did sprawl
Or typing pen to paper.
The songs that tumbled from his throat
Scratched and made his loved ones gloat
At knowing a man so gifted afloat
Could howl and breach no other.

To take that curved and baleful click
And stick it to his temple quick
Just a tiny little flick
Did disappoint his mother.
And now we bid good men goodbye
The Tender Trio aren't all that lie
Tremendous tools of fans do cry
Out for one so so selfish.
Upon the deathbed lived and said
He cannot understand his head
So many realms of compact knowledge
That curls and whirls beneath.
And if one possesses the gift of Art
For it to be received like farts
No joyous mirth intended, start
To understand such dynasty.
That cannot be akin to all who lived
E Pluribus Unum caved and sits
Within the forces of thick cliffs
And tumble down beneath.
So to conclude this wall of words
One ponders the creation of hers
That stands in the form of gender pearls
one cannot comprehend.
A man creates to little avail
That takes away at the pace of a snail
Or quite the contrary, then and there
Just sits within the period.
Time does treat one with many-a-whack

That sits away and cuts no slack
However all may not be Poe
And be known as a man as soon as they
sew.

17th May 2015

Virginity

Come now, take my hand
whispers shuddering upon her neck
kisses poised; body at the ready
aching burning desire seeps inside
walk away, walk away, do prey
now is not the time
no rush needed, my child
no need to slip fingers down those trousers
buttocks pressed into tight skirting dress
this gloss lies outstretched
pulled back, shoved onto cushioned surface
don't tempt her, Magenta, now is not the
time
trust is a wonderful thing
there shall come a time, I'll make her mine
but we have not yet met.

Virginity sits in her solid white box
sheathed in purified robes
she asks; "Why all the fuss?
Why such a large deal to be made?
For I am not tangible, neither audible,
I strike no chord of benevolence.
When time is time and ready is right
I shall come out of my box
But why score points from high to low?
Why judge worth? After all,

I am not tangible."

A guy fucks a girl, he's the Lord of Earl
A girl fucks a guy, kiss respect bye-bye
we are left, wondering how and why
This point was entered
Perhaps the spire of the christian church
is to blame; what a shame for believers
what a shame, but still worse than Mary
Jane
Now we enter a world where baby is choice
Revolution for women everywhere
yet still, looks of scorn and distaste
how could she behave that way?
Plant poisonous words

Slut. Slag. Sket. Skank.
Whore. Hoe. Holy-no-more.

No more worth, for all is plunged
If to give or to keep is a choice
then judge why? Judge not
But still to be done
Glares, hushes, words of regret
Her legs torn apart
"It was your fault" said with a heavy sigh
"You were asking for it."

She should not have worn that tight dress.

She was only asking for it.

9th July 2015

Water

Trickling over sensuous tastebuds
Moulded teardrop of flowing space
Rolling around its carved interior
filled with moistened perfection.
Succulent creamy peace as clarity
serene tilted blue poignant delight
shaped to slither across the river
Entangle to which oceans seek
Volcanoes shall not breach the heat
of echoing reflections that pour from above
Heaven does no shame, put out this flame
Glide with rolls of sliding sweat
sparkle forever in the field of need.

8th July 2015

Why do we write poetry?

Why bother with poetry?
Blabbering on about nonsensical nonsense
Meaningless ultraviolet
Collating a string of words and calling it
aesthetic
Poetry is abstract, useless like Philosophy-
A waste of time, a waste of mind
Impractical, improper, it has no value
In the concrete, consensual world

The poet cannot make any money
Anyone can be a poet
I suppose anyone can be a philosopher
Anyone can be a Shakespeare, Dickinson,
Plath, Blake,

Anyone can be a Descartes, Plato,
Rousseau, Wittgenstein
Or a senior lecturer at the university of tosh

Poetry creates magic in a world full of
boredom
It adds colour and creativity when your
mind is lifeless and dull
The poet and the artist daydream and dwell
Losing hours of sleep to precious minutes of
ink, poised at the paper

Poetry is storytelling without any rules
Poetry is expression
Poetry is kinda like prose but doesn't have
to make sense
Does Zepheniah make sense?
Depends.

Poetry is about interpretation
Poetry is noise and shakes the thunder
Louder than the stomp of an elephant
Poetry cannot be incorrect
Poetry is whatever you want it to be
And that is why
I write
and love
poetry.

2015

A few childhood poems

(2007)

Bedtime

Ah! Bedtime! Best time of the day
Unfortunately time flies by
But I can surely enjoy the time of Troy,
and magic carpets souring high and high.

I love to dream of a funky queen,
and mice riding rats.
And of course there are my best evers,
the dreams to do with cats!

But alas! Something stops this pleasure
the tigers sway away
There's always an uncomfort, meaning:
there's something wrong with the duvet.

I badly need the toilet

I badly need the toilet,
I'm so desperate to pee
I can barely hold it in
In myself I'll probably wee!

I badly need the toilet
I don't know what to do
I'm VERY VERY hungry
but I just want to poo!

I badly need the toilet
but there isn't much point now
it's all faded away
and don't ask me HOW!!

Pure Torture

I prance about to the music
just like I've been told
my fur keeps on falling out
and I'm getting terribly cold.

I try hard not to wonder
about luscious streams
beautiful forests, my friends and family
run around my dreams.

The keeper than raises his bar
and I horridly concentrate
But my mouth is so dry, I wonder
when was the last time I ate?

The children all laugh
and I sob and sob
they all laugh harder
Especially a boy named Rob

And then the devastating show finishes
the keeper sends me to my cage
I curl up to rest, sadly
My fur grimy with age.

7th June 2007

Red Hot Anger!

I sit around, sulking
even though it's a sunny day.
All the children have gone home
there's no one left to play.

I'm really, really bored
feeling angry, nothing to do
Everyone's ignoring me
even if I suddenly poo.

I look forward to the day
when Zarina-me dies
and everyone making my life a misery
bitterly cries.

13th June 2007

Sam

So sad was what happened to Sam,
it's nothing to do with a ram.
He sadly died,
we cried and cried,
staring at the last of his ham.

16th June 2007

Why does everyone hate me so?

Why does everyone hate me so,
makes me very sad.
Everywhere I go, I find people who
drive me crazy, drive me mad.

No where is peaceful,
full of kind people.
All day I'm
full of doom and gloom.

School is useless,
I may have a nice day.
But in butt bloody idiots
Who don't let me have my say!

I always feel like crying
but people's eyes are prying
I hope if they read this poem
they'll realise what's up with me!

12th December 2007

Author's Note

If you enjoyed this poetry collection, please leave a review on Amazon and Goodreads to help support me and independent authors.

My YA novel 'Every Last Psycho' is available to purchase on Amazon as a paperback or Kindle edition.

For more information about my writing, please check out:

zarinamacha.co.uk
thezarinamachablog.co.uk
facebook.com/zarinawriter

And as always, many thanks for reading and purchasing.

20577270R00071

Printed in Great Britain
by Amazon